•Reading is Fun•
•Step 1•

D1744332

in the water

Bob Graham

Blackie

First published in Australia 1984 by
The Five Mile Press

First published in the UK 1986 by
Blackie and Son Ltd
7 Leicester Place, London WC2H 7BP

British Library Cataloguing in Publication Data
Graham, Bob
  In the water.—(Reading is fun)
  1. Readers—1950
  I. Title   II. Series
  428.6   PE1119

  ISBN 0-216-91968-1
  ISBN 0-216-91967-3 Pbk

Printed in Great Britain by
Cambus Litho, East Kilbride

I can wash Jim.

I can float.

I can dive.

I can swim.

I can row.

I can splash.

I can paddle.

I can fish.

General advice to adults with young children learning to read.

1   Conversation is vital for children learning to read: talk with your child as much as possible. Listen carefully to what children say to you and answer their questions as fully as you can.

2   Read and teach children nursery rhymes – they enjoy the sounds and rhythms of the words and it doesn't matter if they don't understand them all.

3   If possible, read aloud to your child at least once a day. Children who are used to sharing the pleasures of books with an adult have a head start with reading because they know the enjoyment it can offer. They come to know a great deal about books and stories by listening to them read aloud (particularly from picture books), by playing out stories, by telling stories and listening to them on radio, TV or cassette.

4   Let your children see you reading too. If children see their parents absorbed in books and enjoying them, they are likely to feel that reading is something they want to enjoy – after all, most children want to be like their parents.

5   The beginner reader needs to know a lot of things that we take for granted. For example, that a book starts from the front and is read page by page to the back; that words are read from left to right across the pages and that lines are read from top to bottom. So, when you read with a young child, have him/her on your lap so he/she can follow the words. Read the story slowly, running your finger under the words as you say them. You can do this several times and then perhaps ask your child to join in. But never force children: praise and encouragement are essential.

6   Never make comparisons with the progress of other children. Just as they learn to walk and talk in their own time, so children learn to read at different rates.

7   When a child is reading to you, don't worry about correcting him/her if the meaning is right. If it doesn't make sense, most children will stop reading anyway.

8　If, in the very early stages a child doesn't know a word, tell him/her what it is. Later on, try reading the phrase immediately before the unknown word then stop and see if the child can fill it in. If this doesn't help, go on a bit beyond the unknown word and see if he/she can guess it from the rest of the sentence(s). Perhaps the illustration can give a clue. If in doubt though, always tell your child the word.

9　Use the local library to supplement your child's growing collection of books.

10　Don't forget the written language that is all round us: TV ads, labels on sweets, packets, street signs, shops, etc. Read them with your children.

11　Remember too that writing helps with reading. It reminds children that written words mean things, that words go from left to right and top to bottom and that letters are ways of writing down sounds. Writing their own books, first by dictating them to you, then later, on their own, helps children to discover how stories work and encourages them to see themselves as writers as well as readers.

12　Most schools now welcome parents in to discuss reading and how they can help. So, if your child has started school, take every opportunity to talk with his/her teacher; it will give both teacher and child the feeling that you value and support their work and helps you as a parent to understand what your child is talking about.

JILL BENNETT